Lucasville Legends is published by Lucasville Media
an imprint of JL dub Media, Inc.
9255 Towne Centre Drive, Suite 500, San Diego, CA 92121

No part of this publication may be reproduced in whole or in part,
or stored in a retrieval system, or transmitted in any form or by any means,
electronic, mechanical, photocopying, recording, or otherwise,
without written permission of the publisher.

For information regarding permission, write to
JL dub Media, Inc.
9255 Towne Centre Drive, Suite 500, San Diego, CA 92121
www.Lucasville.com

Lucasville is a registered trademark of JL dub Media, Inc.

Printed in the United States of America

**Editorial Credits**
Tom Kerns, Competition Aerobatic Pilot
Sarah M. Crookston, Reading Specialist

**Photo Credits**
Coastal Carolina Air Show. 14b, 15a, 20c
Cook, Clark. 32-33
Donath, Devon. 14a, 20a, 24
Gibson, Wes. 5
GoPro 17b, 29ab
Halseth, Nick. Covers, 2-3, 8-9, 27b, 28, 30
Jossi, Alex. 15b
Lopez, Stephen. 31b
Wilson, Janet. 6-7, 13ab, 16ab, 17a, 18ab, 19, 26a

Morrone, Domenico. 21
Nayak, P. Sachin. 26b
Photoz by Liza. 25b, 27a, Back
Pope, Conrad. 20b
Szmiot, Nick. 25a
Turrill, Keith. 10-11
Uttecht, Dani. 12ab, 22-23
Watson, Gavan. 31a

Publisher's Cataloging-in-Publication data

Wilson, Janet L.
    Michael's stunt plane / Janet Wilson.
    p. cm.
    ISBN 978-0-9834110-2-4
    Series : Lucasville Legends.

1. Stunt flying --Fiction. 2. Airplanes --Fiction. 3. Stunt flying --Juvenile fiction.
4. Airplanes --Juvenile fiction. I. Series. II. Title.

PZ7.W6843 Mi 2011
[Fic]                                                                      2011906722
The publisher does not endorse products whose logos may appear in images in this book.

# Michael's
# Stunt Plane

Janet Wilson

Hi! My name is Michael Wiskus and I am the pilot of the Lucas Oil stunt plane. My first airplane ride was in a stunt plane when I was ten years old.

6

The pilot did loops and barrel rolls.
My mother was terrified, but I loved it!
After that first ride, I always dreamed
about having my own plane.

My first job was at the local airport.
I washed planes and cleaned out hangars.
I saved all of my money for flying lessons. On my
17th birthday, I earned my pilots license.

**Rudder**
used to turn the
plane left or right

**Canopy**
slides shut to
protect the pilot

**Tail Wheel**
used to support
and steer the tail

**Body**
Model: **Pitts Special S-1-11B**
Frame: **steel tubing**
Structure: **aluminum and
wood stringers**
Material: **synthetic canvas**
Wing Span: **18 feet**

# Plane

**Engine**
Type: **Barrett Performance**
Horsepower: **330**
Fuel: **100 octane aviation**
Capacity: **26 gallons**

**Air Scoops**
used to force air
into the engine

A biplane is a fixed-wing aircraft with two main wings. Two wings create more lift than a single wing plane. A short wingspan makes a stunt plane easy to maneuver.

**Front Landing Gear**
main support during
take offs and landings

**Propeller**
spins 2,950
times a minute

**Struts**
permit a light,
but very strong
wing structure

# Stunt

**Four Ailerons**
used to control the
roll of the plane

**Smoke**
produced by injecting
fog oil into the hot
engine exhaust

Stunt planes are also designed to fly inverted.
Special pumps move the fuel and oil
to the engine when flying upside down.

Every morning I think the same thing . . .
"This looks like a great day to go flying!"

Today I will be performing my favorite stunts
in an air show. My plane is checked carefully.

I review the flight plans for the air show.
I am performing stunts in the morning.
In the afternoon, I am flying with the
U.S. Navy Blue Angels!

This *really* is a great day
to go flying!

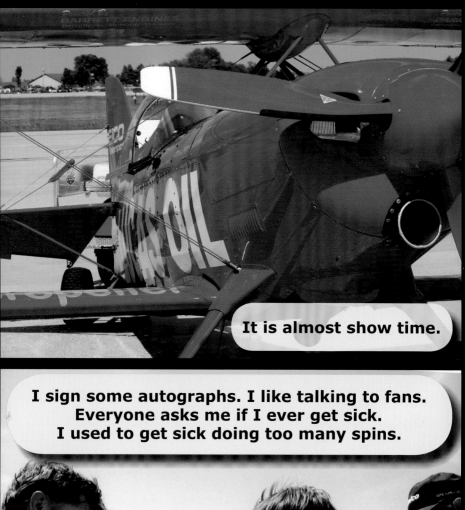

It is almost show time.

I sign some autographs. I like talking to fans.
Everyone asks me if I ever get sick.
I used to get sick doing too many spins.

Throwing up when spinning
makes a big mess!

Preparing to be a stunt pilot is hard work. There is a special way to breathe when doing stunts and I exercise to keep my body strong. I have trained myself not to be sick!

The TV station does an interview. Many people are interested in stunt flying.

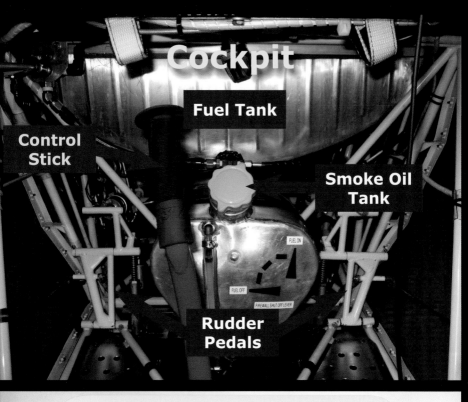

The seat belt is a 5-point harness with padded shoulders. The padding cushions the G-forces.

The G-forces will quickly change from negative 7 to positive 9! Negative G-forces pull me out of my seat. Positive G-forces push me down into my seat.

Control Stick

Hand Throttle and Smoke Button

Are you wondering where my helmet is? This may be a surprise, but these stunts are more strenuous when I am wearing a helmet. The G-forces will make my helmet feel like it weighs 10 pounds!

17

The **maneuver** list is taped to the dashboard. My shoelaces are taped down with duct tape. I do not want them to catch on anything.

When performing stunts, I use a triangle called a sighting device. When I am flying level, the center bar will line up with the **horizon**.

**This is my maneuver list.**
**A stunt begins at the solid round dot**
**and ends at the short vertical line.**

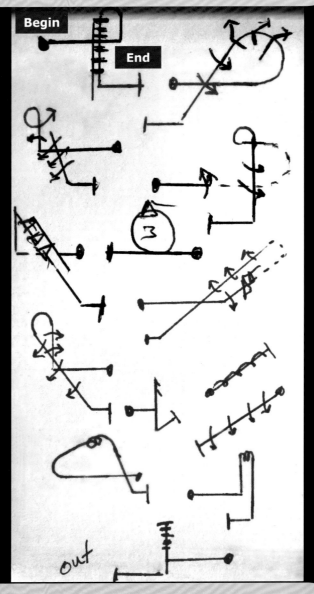

Begin

End

out

**Inverted flight (negative G-force)**
**is shown as a dashed line.**
**The arrows show a rolling maneuver.**

I pull the **control stick** back and the plane lifts up.

The freedom I feel when I am flying is awesome. Flying is my favorite thing to do.

20

This stunt is called the Tail Slide. I climb vertically until the plane loses momentum. I fall backwards, tail first, until the nose drops.

I start thinking about my next stunt. I will be performing loops and spins and the plane will be **inverted**.

Pressing the smoke button on the throttle sends fog oil into the exhaust. Fog oil creates the smoke trail.

This stunt is the Spiral Up, Spiral Down, Snap Roll. Woooo HOOOO!

When planes are inverted, their controls are reversed. Now I must remember to *push* the control stick forward to go up.

I finish my morning performance with two single-winged planes. We are flying in formation.

The morning show was great!
Now I think about the afternoon show. I will be flying with the world famous Blue Angels.

The Blue Angels are the U.S. Navy's flight demonstration **squadron**. Their planes are F/A-18 Hornets. How cool is that?

I take off and fly around the airport.

Two Blue Angels join me and we begin our routine. I can hear their powerful jet engines.

I flip over and we are flying in formation.

Wow! We just zoomed past the air show at 280 mph. Those jets are amazing!

I flip back over and exit the formation. Now I will begin my solo stunt routine.

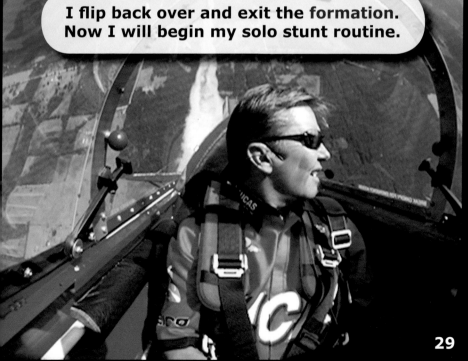

Performing back-to-back stunts is stressful. Pulling so many G's might cause me to blackout. I must control my breathing and tighten my neck and stomach muscles. Hang on!

One of my favorite stunts is to stall my plane. It looks like I am falling out of the sky!

This stunt is a Double Forward Somersault. It ends in a tight loop and the plane is inverted. It feels like I am on a wild roller coaster ride!

I stay focused during each maneuver and I always keep an eye on the ground.

My final stunt is a High Alpha. Sometimes this is called my "photo pass" because I wave good-bye to the crowd.

LUCASVILLE Legends ON THE EDGE

# Vocabulary

**aileron** [**EY**-l*uh*-ron] - a movable surface at the edge of a wing that controls the roll of the plane

**control stick** [k*uh*n-**TROHL** stik] - used to control the movements of the plane

**G-force** [**G** fohrs] - a unit to measure the force of gravity

**formation** [fawr-**MAY**-sh*uh*n] - the formal arrangement of many planes acting as a unit

**horizon** [h*uh*-**RAHY**-z*uh*n] - the line that forms between the earth and sky

**horsepower** [**HAWRS**-pou-er] - a unit to measure the power of an engine

**invert** [in-**VERT**] - to turn upside down

**maneuver** [m*uh*-**NOO**-ver] - planned movement of an airplane in flight

**somersault** [**SUHM**-er-sawlt] - a movement where the plane rolls end over end

**strenuous** [**STREN**-yoo-*uhs*] - requiring the use of great energy or effort

**squadron** [**SKWOD**-r*uh*n] - a portion of a naval fleet

**wingspan** [**WING**-span] - the distance between the wing tips

**vertical** [**VUR**-ti-k*uh*l] - upright position